Mort Künstler's
CIVIL WAR

★ ★ ★

THE SOUTH

★ ★ ★

Mort Künstler's

CIVIL WAR

☆ ☆ ☆

☆ ☆ ☆

Mort Künstler

RUTLEDGE HILL PRESS®

Nashville, Tennessee

A Thomas Nelson Company

Published by Rutledge Hill Press, a Thomas Nelson Company,
P.O. Box 141000, Nashville, Tennessee 37214.

Jacket and text design by Bruce Gore/Gore Studio, Inc.

Library of Congress Cataloging-in-Publication Data

Künstler, Mort.
    [Civil War]
    Mort Künstler's Civil War : the South / Mort Künstler.
       p. cm.
    ISBN 1-55853-478-4
    1. United States—History—Civil War, 1861–1865—Pictorial works—
Catalogs. 2. United States—History—Civil War, 1861–1865—Art and the
war—Catalogs. 3. Confederate States of America—Pictorial works—Catalogs.
4. Confederate States of America—Pictorial works—Catalogs. 5. Künstler,
Mort—Catalogs.   I. Title.
E468.7.K86   1997
973.7—dc21
                                                                97-9407
                                                                CIP

Printed in Mexico
3 4 5 6 7 8 9 — 05 04 03 02 01 00

Especially for
ANDREW *and* LAURA

☆ ☆ ☆

Contents

★ ★ ★

Introduction	8
"There Stands Jackson Like a Stone Wall"	10
Southern Stars	16
Until We Meet Again	24
Confederate Winter	32
Gen. Stonewall Jackson Enters Winchester, Va.	40
"I Will Be Moving Within the Hour"	48
The Commanders of Manassas	56
Night Crossing	64
Lee at Fredericksburg	72
"…War Is So Terrible"	80
The Review at Moss Neck	88
Wayside Farewell	96
Winter Riders	106
Confederate Sunset	114
Model Partnership	122
The Last Council	130
The Grand Review	136
The Loneliness of Command	144
The High Water Mark	152
"It's All My Fault"	160
Confederate Christmas	168
Thunder in the Valley	176
"We Still Love You, General Lee"	184
Acknowledgments	192

Introduction

ALL ARTISTS thrive on applause. Until 1988 my "applause" was limited to the twenty or thirty people who bought my paintings every two years or so from one of my exhibitions at Hammer Galleries in New York City.

In 1988 my painting *The High Water Mark* was made into a limited-edition print by American Print Gallery in Gettysburg. This multiplied my audience one-hundred-fold. Sixty-eight prints and three books on the Civil War have followed since then. The books alone have sold more than three hundred thousand copies. Truly, I never dreamed of that much applause.

With this vast new group of people responding to my work, I was suddenly able to see which of my paintings were the most popular by noting those that sold out most quickly and by watching the secondary market created after the print sold out. People seemed to respond most ardently to Confederate subjects. I responded to that demand by painting so many Confederate subjects that I am very often called a "southern" artist. This I accept with pride.

Many times I hear northerners say, "They're still fighting the Civil War in the South." My response is that they are not fighting it, they are remembering it. Southerners have good reasons for remembering it. The war was fought in the South. They are reminded every day on their way to work, when they pass battlefield sites, military parks, and cemeteries. More importantly, southerners, especially in the small cities and towns and in rural areas, tend to remain in the same area for generations. They trace their ancestry back to the war, while many northerners, especially from the large urban centers, trace their ancestry back to Ellis Island and respond to that imagery.

This new book, having a southern viewpoint, attempts to take the viewer on a gallery tour of some of my favorite Confederate paintings and points out in words and pictures that these paintings are not done in a flash of inspiration. One painting takes weeks, even months of research, preliminary planning, sketching, and painting. For the first time I have tried to show some of the "behind the scenes" work that is involved.

All of the leading players are featured in the following pages. Johnny Reb is present, but most of all we see two Southern generals, Stonewall Jackson and Robert E. Lee. My fascination with these two Confederate icons resulted in the book *Jackson and Lee*, published in 1995.

Of the twenty-three paintings that make up this book, nine have never been published in any book. All of the paintings are done with a reverence for detail, authenticity, and most of all, the people of this most American of all wars.

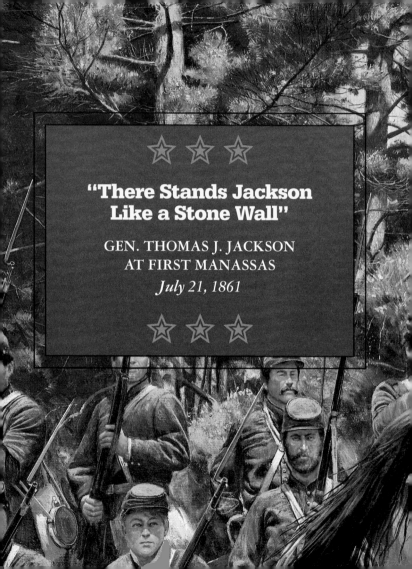

"There Stands Jackson Like a Stone Wall"

GEN. THOMAS J. JACKSON
AT FIRST MANASSAS
July 21, 1861

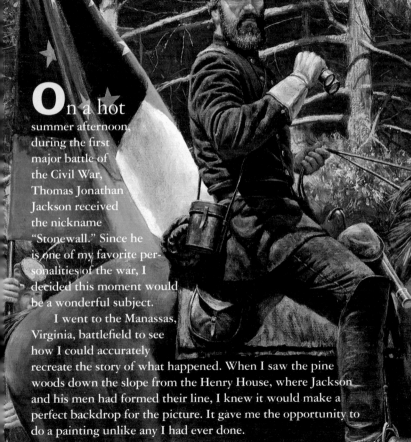

On a hot summer afternoon, during the first major battle of the Civil War, Thomas Jonathan Jackson received the nickname "Stonewall." Since he is one of my favorite personalities of the war, I decided this moment would be a wonderful subject.

I went to the Manassas, Virginia, battlefield to see how I could accurately recreate the story of what happened. When I saw the pine woods down the slope from the Henry House, where Jackson and his men had formed their line, I knew it would make a perfect backdrop for the picture. It gave me the opportunity to do a painting unlike any I had ever done.

The battle on July 21, 1861, was going against the Confederates. Jackson and his men were in position on Henry House Hill, but the fighting had not yet reached them. Two brigades of Southerners were caught in the initial Federal attack just below Jackson. One of the brigade commanders, Barnard Bee, rallied his troops by pointing toward Jackson and saying, "There is Jackson standing like a stone wall. Let us determine to die here, and we will conquer." Bee was wounded shortly after making that statement and died the next day, but Jackson and his men did indeed stand "like a stone wall" against the Federal advance. The Southerners rallied and the Northern army abandoned the battlefield in chaos.

Jackson, of course, is the center of interest. He is dressed in his old blue Virginia Military Institute uniform and forage cap, scanning the crest of Henry House Hill to the west, anticipating his first glimpse of Union troops. Behind him is a line of Virginia infantry, many wearing the frock coat of the Virginia militia, which was later abandoned. The men are armed with the Model 1842 musket. With bayonets fixed, they must have been an awesome sight.

The soldier directly behind Jackson holds the first national flag of the Confederacy. Its similarity to the U.S. flag, with its field of white stars on a blue field in the corner and alternating red and white bars on the body of the flag, created much confusion during the early months of the war.

Also contributing to the battlefield chaos were the blue uniforms from the "old army" that were worn by many Confederates. This, too, would change over time as uniforms were standardized to gray and blue.

I wanted to capture the moment just before Jackson and his men were engaged by the Federals. I wanted to catch that last moment of the calm before the storm—the second that a legend was born.

Southern Stars

KERNSTOWN, VA.

Winter 1862

For years I envisioned this painting. It was a snowy night scene with a group of horsemen riding by a church just as services ended. With the church dominating the scene, I pictured the congregation milling around the church doors to watch the passing soldiers.

For some time I searched for a charming country church in a setting that matched my imagination. Finally, I "discovered" the Opequon Presbyterian Church in Kernstown, Virginia, near historic Winchester. The church building was on the site of the 1862 battle of Kernstown. Area historians C. Langdon Gordon, Ben Ritter, and Maral Kalbian told me of the church's history.

The original Opequon Church was severely damaged during the battle of Kernstown and was later destroyed by fire in 1873. The present building was constructed on the foundation of the original structure and used windows of the same shape and size as the Civil

War–era building. Unfortunately, no image of the original church exists, so I based this painting on the present-day building and tried to capture the qualities and atmosphere of the church during the war.

The worlds of war and peace collide in this tranquil winter landscape. A mother and baby are prominent among the churchgoers, representing the homes and families left behind by the young men who went to war. The churchgoers on the stoop silently watch the soldiers pass.

The horsemen, possibly envious of the inner warmth of the church—both physical and emotional—neither greet nor wave to the civilians as they continue on their mission. Perhaps they sense the irony of their presence near this symbol of faith and peace.

Preliminary sketch

Until We Meet Again

JACKSON'S HEADQUARTERS
Winchester, Va.
Winter 1862

The inspiration and idea for this painting came about through a series of circumstances. My original painting *Jackson Enters Winchester* was purchased by the Farmers and Merchants Bank of Winchester. The bank's chief executive officer, Wil Feltner, then asked if I might be interested in painting a companion piece.

During a visit to Stonewall Jackson's headquarters in Winchester, I learned that the historic building had never been depicted in a painting. Here was my opportunity.

No fighting occurred at Jackson's winter headquarters, so I chose to illustrate a tranquil snow scene similar to my painting *Confederate Winter*. Walking around the headquarters, the former Lewis T. Moore home, I found the most interesting side of the building was the original front. Research told me that, aside from the entrance, the only major changes made since Jackson's time were the addition of two dormers on the second floor.

It was in Winchester that Jackson's wife, Mary Anna, joined him for the winter of 1861–62. They were very devoted to each other, and she often walked to his headquarters with a basket of food for his supper.

The scene I chose to depict shows Jackson saying good-bye to Mary Anna. As the general's entourage waits, the couple walks a few steps away for some parting words in private.

The general's uniform is blue rather than Confederate gray, a holdover from his days at the Virginia Military Institute. It conforms to the 1850 uniform regulations for the Virginia militia and, except for the buttons, is the "old army" uniform.

Jackson's staff witness this tender moment. Maj. Henry Kyd Douglas, the mounted officer on the extreme left of the painting, later gained fame as one of Jackson's biographers. On foot and immediately to Douglas's right is Lt. Col. William Allan, Jackson's chief of artillery. Directly behind him, a mounted trooper chats with Capt. Jed Hotchkiss, topographical engineer and noted mapmaker.

Just to the left of the stairs is Dr. Hunter McGuire, Jackson's medical chief, who later made his home in Winchester. Alongside Dr. McGuire is Lt. Alexander "Sandie" Pendleton, wearing a red artillery officer's kepi. On the right of the stairs, Maj. Rev. Robert L. Dabney, in winter cape and coat, waits with Capt. J. G. Morrison.

To the right of Morrison, a mounted trooper of Jackson's cavalry escort carries the standard of the first national flag. Maj. D. B. Bridgeforth is on the extreme right. The rest of the officers and men wait patiently, some turning away out of respect for Jackson's privacy during this unexpected show of tenderness.

The Jacksons' only child, Julia, was born the following November. I was privileged to know her daughter, Mrs. Julia Christian Preston.

Figure sketch

Jackson's winter headquarters as it looks today.

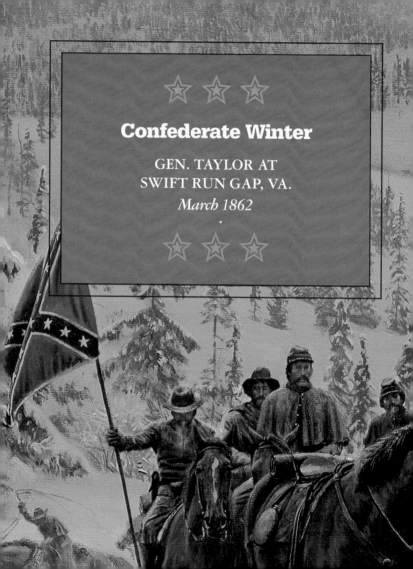

Confederate Winter

GEN. TAYLOR AT
SWIFT RUN GAP, VA.

March 1862

My painting *Confederate Winter* came about in an unusual way. I almost always take a certain event, discover the facts I need for the basic work, and then try to create a good painting. In this case, I worked in reverse. I had wanted to do a snow scene with a Civil War theme as well as a long view, or "vista," for some time. I was able to accomplish all of this in *Confederate Winter*.

With few exceptions, no battles were fought during the winter season. There were, however, a few necessary cold marches. So I looked for information on troop movements during inclement weather.

After some research, I learned that Gen. Richard Taylor led his Louisiana Brigade and some Virginia troops through Swift Run Gap, Virginia, in March 1862. Marching under foul weather conditions, they reinforced Stonewall Jackson's army for the upcoming spring Shenandoah Valley campaign. This was the basic plot I needed for my painting.

Starting with the view and the knowledge of where the old road lay in the gap, I now had my long mountain vista *and* snow! Taylor (holding the map) and his staff lead the first infantry regiments, followed by a battery of artillery struggling through the snow and mud on the uphill course of the road. The next regiments follow. Finally, in the far distance, supply wagons can be seen bringing up the rear.

Taylor's likeness is based on a contemporary photograph. The idea of a twilight scene is something that has always appealed to me, because it is difficult to illustrate. By using the lantern, I was able to exploit the contrasting warm light to accentuate the center of interest and emphasize the cold evening lighting effect.

It is not an easy task to create a war painting that projects peace and tranquillity, but I believe this one does.

Figure sketch

Compositional sketch

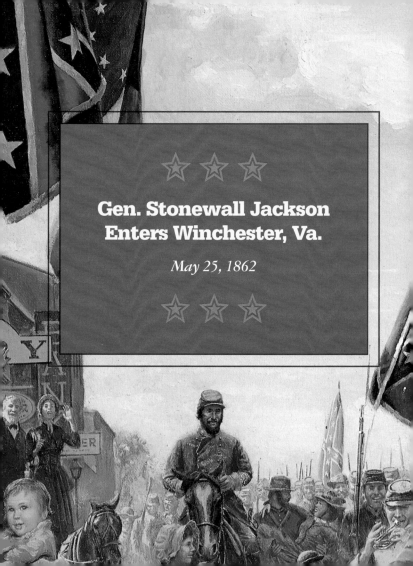

Gen. Stonewall Jackson Enters Winchester, Va.

May 25, 1862

The inspiration for this painting came
from Stonewall Jackson himself. In a letter to his wife he men-
tioned, "I do not remember ever having seen such rejoicing. Our
entrance into Winchester was one of the most stirring scenes of
my life."

With this as my starting point, I went to Winchester to
research the painting. Rebecca Ebert and Ben Ritter of the
Winchester Library and the Winchester Historical Society
offered immeasurable help. Their archives held old photographs and records that guided me in portray-
ing the town as it was in 1862.

The May 25, 1862, battle at
Winchester (there were two
other battles for Win-
chester later in the
war) pitted
Jackson
against

Union Gen. Nathaniel P. Banks as part of a critical, month-long campaign for control of the Shenandoah Valley. The Confederacy had lost the Mississippi Valley and could not afford to lose the Shenandoah.

The Confederate commander outmaneuvered the Northerners to gain an easy victory in Front Royal on May 23. The two armies then raced toward Winchester. Jackson's troops completed the unforgiving 160-mile march, fighting two battles along the way. On May 24, his men captured a Federal wagon train, and the next day the Southerners defeated Banks's main force at Winchester, which then retreated toward the Potomac.

Between his victories at Front Royal and Winchester,

Jackson had captured two thousand prisoners, nine thousand rifles, and an abundance of food and medical supplies. On May 25, his men entered the town, and the city's population turned out to welcome the victorious little army.

In painting this triumphal parade, I placed the key focus on Taylor's Hotel, a famous local landmark that Banks had used as his headquarters. The building has changed quite a bit since 1862 and now houses a McCrory's department store. I based the other buildings and signs on information gleaned from the archives and other sources. The Russell and Green Dry Goods Store stands next to Taylor's Hotel, with Bell's Book Store adjacent to that. Another hotel, The Washington, stands across the street. A dry goods store, farther up the street, and other shops are placed as accurately as my research allowed. The brick sidewalk and stone curbing in the lower left corner still exist on some city streets today.

Of the four mounted officers, Jackson is the center of interest, deliberately silhouetted against the sky, with his closest staff members nearby. On the left, riding in the background, is Maj. Robert Dabney. The officer to Jackson's right, waving his hat to friends on the hotel balcony, is Dr. Hunter McGuire. The last officer is Maj. Henry Kyd Douglas.

Jackson and his troops entered Winchester on May 25 at about 10 o'clock in the morning. I was not able to visit the area on that particular date to note the lighting effect at that time of year. When I did visit Winchester toward the end of July, it was one month past the spring equinox and the lighting was virtually the same as on May 25.

Figure sketch

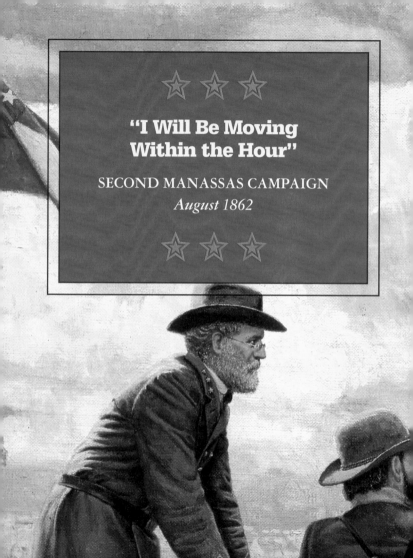

"I Will Be Moving Within the Hour"

SECOND MANASSAS CAMPAIGN
August 1862

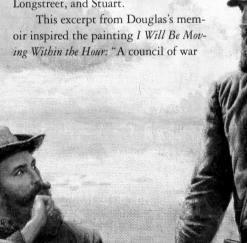

The strategic planning that always preceded Lee and Jackson's great victories is fascinating to me. My 1990 painting *The Last Council* depicted one of their dramatic conferences, and I had been searching for a similar event to paint when I settled on this scene.

I learned of another conference from the classic memoir by Maj. Henry Kyd Douglas, one of Stonewall Jackson's staff officers. Longstreet's autobiography, *From Manassas to Appomattox*, mentions the same meeting, as does Douglas Southall Freeman's *Lee's Lieutenants*. The incident occurred at the beginning of the Second Manassas campaign in August 1862. It was a unique, crucial battle conference that brought together Lee, Jackson, Longstreet, and Stuart.

This excerpt from Douglas's memoir inspired the painting *I Will Be Moving Within the Hour:* "A council of war

was held at the General's headquarters that afternoon. It was a curious scene. A table was placed almost in the middle of a field, with not even a tree within hearing. General Lee sat at the table on which was spread a map. General Longstreet sat on his right, General Stuart on his left, and General Jackson stood opposite him; these four and no more. The consultation was a brief one. . . . As it closed I was called by General Jackson and I heard the only sentence of that consultation that I ever heard reported. It was uttered by the secretive Jackson and it was, 'I will be moving within the hour.'"

In the painting, Lee, Jackson, Longstreet, and Stuart are seen at the little table in the middle of the grassy field, surrounded by terrain typical of the Manassas region. Nearby, above Lee's headquarters tent, the first national flag of the Confederacy is ruffled by a breeze. Beside it is the Confederate battle flag. The elevated viewpoint provides the opportunity to depict Lee's great Army of Northern Virginia—troops, tents, wagons, and other equipment of war—sprawled across the scenic Virginia countryside.

This painting is part of a series called *Jackson and Lee: Legends in Gray*, which depicts key scenes in the remarkable wartime relationship between the two great Confederate generals.

Portrait sketch

The Commanders of Manassas

GENS. LEE, LONGSTREET, AND JACKSON
August 29, 1862

I am
always looking for significant
moments that have been overlooked
by other Civil War artists. The event
I depicted here is well documented,
and it gave me an opportunity to por-
tray Stonewall Jackson, Robert E. Lee,
and James Longstreet. The three
were brought together on August
29, 1862, just before the battle of
Second Manassas.

The Confederates had divided
their forces five days earlier.
Jackson surprised a Federal
force at Bristoe Station, seiz-
ing a large quantity of food.
Then he encountered Union
Gen. John Pope at the old
battlefield near Manassas
Junction. After two days
of fighting, Lee and
thirty thousand Confed-
erates arrived and
counterattacked. The

overwhelmed Federals retreated in chaos, with the Army of Northern Virginia in close pursuit.

I portrayed the generals' reunion as I envisioned it: Lee and Longstreet joining Jackson in the early afternoon on a warm August day. From their elevated position, Jackson points out the disposition of his lines, and they discuss the most effective deployment of Lee's fresh troops.

In addition to showing the three legendary commanders and their staffs, I had the opportunity to paint a bright sunlit scene, which would be in contrast to many of my Civil War pieces. Another challenge would be my treatment of the long vista. I recreated it using topographical, vegetation, and battle maps, all of which were supplied by Jim Phelps and Ray Brown of the Manassas National Military Park.

In the distance is the unfinished railroad cut, and in the middle of the painting is the Warrenton Pike. Today, trees block this view of the battlefield, but the Park Service may clear away the woods in the future so visitors can have the same view the generals had in 1862.

The area is Stuart's Hill. I used a partly fallen oak as the setting to add to the drama. The generals would quite naturally have looked for shade to escape the summer sun and camouflage their position from enemy observers. The black-eyed susans are typical field flowers in that area in August.

Jackson's pose is characteristic of him, as is his attire—dust covered and field worn. His uniform offers a contrast to Lee's informal colonel's coat and Longstreet's gold-braided frock coat.

Mixed media study

Night Crossing

LEE AND JACKSON
September 18, 1862

Night *Crossing* is one of the most challenging paintings I have done in years. The idea for the painting came from rereading Douglas Southall Freeman's matchless biography of Robert E. Lee. I was captivated by his account of Lee's army crossing the Potomac River after the battle of Sharpsburg (known as Antietam in the North). I realized his description of the scene offered a perfect opportunity for a powerful picture containing several artistically challenging elements: darkness, water, and contrasting light.

Lee had hoped to end the war with a battle on Northern soil. Now he stood on the banks of the Potomac, watching his army withdraw into Virginia. Beside him was the silent Stonewall Jackson, who had done so much to assist Lee in the awful fighting waged two days earlier in Maryland.

These were the final moments of Lee's first invasion of the North. His highest hopes had been for a great Southern victory that would prompt European recognition of the Confederate States. The campaign ended, however, with the bloodiest single day of the war. Lee lost one-fourth of his army, and instead of a victory, he had to settle for a stalemate on the banks of Antietam Creek. Braced for an attack the next day that never came, the gray legions withdrew.

Once the army was safely across the river in his beloved Virginia, Lee allowed himself to relax. He and his men would fight again.

The difficulty of painting the river was a challenge that was complicated further by the torchlight used by the troops. The bright light was a dramatic contrast to the cool, blue night. The scene holds great drama, pathos, and energy—horses splashing in excitement, artillery caissons backing up, confusion and chaos—all supervised by a calm, determined Lee. Beside him, Jackson silently surveys the action as his quartermaster, Col. John Harmon, tries to undo the confusion and supervise the crossing.

In contrast to the energy and action in the background, I portrayed Lee and Jackson as calm commanders, reflecting the confidence and discipline that characterized their leadership.

Compositional sketch

Mixed media study

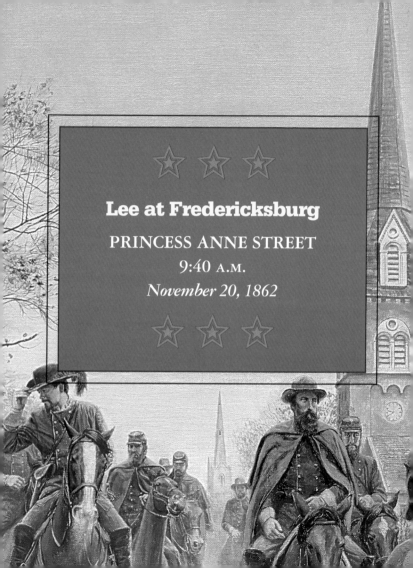

Lee at Fredericksburg

PRINCESS ANNE STREET

9:40 A.M.

November 20, 1862

I had wanted to do a painting of Fredericksburg, Virginia, for some time. Not only was it the site of a very important battle of the Civil War, it was also a beautiful city. When I learned that no artist had ever painted Lee and Longstreet at Fredericksburg, that was the only impetus I needed to begin the project.

As I walked through Fredericksburg, the appeal and beauty of the city became apparent. The steeples of Princess Anne Street pulled me like a magnet. Once I had walked along this main city street, I knew I had found the setting for my painting.

By facing north, near the Mason's Hall, I was able to get all three steeples into view. On the right is the brick courthouse steeple. Further down the street and in the center of the painting is the towering steeple of St. George's Episcopal Church, virtually unchanged since the war. In the far distance, one sees the Baptist church steeple. The building on the extreme left was a residence at the time and still exists, almost the same as it was in 1862.

I felt the best moment to depict would be one showing Lee and Longstreet together. I learned that on the morning of November 20, 1862, both generals rode down Princess Anne Street with their entourages. The citizenry, made up primarily of women, children, and old men, were surprised and delighted to see the famous legends in person. The people believed their saviors had arrived.

The center of interest is, of course, Lee riding on Traveller. To his right is Longstreet, whom Lee had ordered to Fredericksburg. Immediately behind them is a trooper carrying a Confederate battle flag. Directly under the flag is Col. Charles Marshall, Lee's aide-de-camp throughout the war. In back of the flag, between Marshall and Lee, is Col. James Corley, chief quartermaster. To the left of the clock on the St. George's steeple is Lee's medical director, Lafayette Guild. Riding in front of him and to the left of the steeple is Maj. Charles Venable. To his left, tipping his hat to a group of young female admirers, is Col. Walter Taylor. To Taylor's right and directly behind him is Col. Briscoe Baldwin, chief of ordnance. Other officers of both staffs and escort troopers follow.

The mood of the civilians changed dramatically in the next forty-eight hours. A Union army encamped on the other side of the Rappahannock River and warned the people of an imminent bombardment, which began on the morning of December 11. Fredericksburg would never be the same.

Partially finished painting

Princess Anne Street as it looks today.

"...War Is So Terrible"

LONGSTREET AND LEE
December 13, 1862

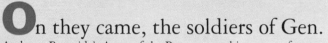

On they came, the soldiers of Gen. Ambrose Burnside's Army of the Potomac, rushing wave after wave into the massed fire of Robert E. Lee's Army of Northern Virginia at Marye's Heights. It was a courageous, magnificent, and futile assault, and it made the battle of Fredericksburg on December 13, 1862, one of the bloodiest engagements of the Civil War. It was also one of Lee's greatest victories.

Accompanied by Gen. James Longstreet, Lee watched the battle unfold from Lee's Hill, a ridge east of Marye's Heights that overlooked the city. Fog shrouded the ridge. For several long, tense moments, the two could not see what was happening to the right side of their line, which was obscured by a stand of timber.

What they

could see was troubling. Northern troops poured into the woods; wounded Southerners streamed out. Couriers reported savage fighting, and captured Confederates were seen being marched to the Federal rear.

Then the Rebel yell broke above the battle's clamor—an "unearthly, fiendish" cheer—and Lee saw the Federals pour from the woods in retreat, pursued by his wildly shouting soldiers.

The moment symbolized both the glory and the gore of war—simultaneously stirring and horrible. Lee turned to Longstreet and in one terse statement placed both the hope and the horror of war in proper perspective: "It is well that war is so terrible—we should grow too fond of it." These words sum up the character of the man in one sentence. In spite of the great victory he had just gained, he never lost sight of the horrors of war.

I visited both Lee's Hill and Marye's Heights and was assisted immeasurably by Frank O'Reilly, the National Park Service historian at Fredericksburg. Famed author and historian James I. Robertson Jr. also helped in determining the time of day and weather conditions of that morning.

In addition to Longstreet, Lee, and their attending staffs, I was also able to incorporate the gun positions and crews into the painting. Since Federal artillery had shelled Lee's Hill, I added twisted and wrecked trees to introduce depth, authenticity, and the feeling of death.

Conceptual sketch (above). Mixed media study (right).

The Review at Moss Neck

FREDERICKSBURG, VA.

January 20, 1863

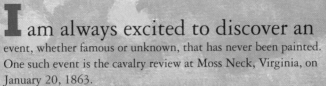

I am always excited to discover an event, whether famous or unknown, that has never been painted. One such event is the cavalry review at Moss Neck, Virginia, on January 20, 1863.

I came across a reference to it in Henry Kyd Douglas's biography of Stonewall Jackson, *I Rode with Stonewall*, in which he noted that Jackson and Lee reviewed Stuart's troops at the plantation.

To confirm this information, I contacted James I. Robertson Jr., today's foremost authority on Jackson. Not only did he verify the event, but he cross-referenced it with other sources, placing Rooney Lee and James Longstreet there was well. With Professor Robertson's help, I was able to obtain photographs of the Moss Neck mansion the way it looked at the time. It still exists and has changed little in appearance since the war.

Moss Neck is ten miles south of Fredericksburg, site of one of the greatest victories for Lee's Army of Northern Virginia in December 1862. Jackson established his headquarters there and occupied a wood-frame building near the main house.

In mid-January 1863 the Confederates discovered the Union army was then moving to cross the Rappahannock River to strike at Lee again. Lee rode to Moss Neck, where he found Jackson and Longstreet disagreeing over how to respond to this unexpected winter offensive. Lee settled their dispute and reviewed options with them for the next two days. They need not have worried. The Federals' plans were frustrated when rain and snow made the roads impassable.

With the threat of attack removed, Lee reviewed the troops before leaving. The men he inspected were commanded by his son, Gen. William Henry Fitzhugh "Rooney" Lee. In the painting, the troopers are lined up on the left with the Confederate battle flag, the Virginia flag, and the first national flag of the Confederate States. They sport a variety of firearms from carbines to sawed-off shotguns.

Lee is at the head of the inspection party, wearing a blue cape. He is flanked by Jackson on his left, directly under the battle flag. Rooney Lee is on the far left, closest to his troops. On the right, in the red-lined cape and plumed hat, riding his favorite black charger, is Gen. Jeb Stuart. Longstreet, Lee's "Old War Horse," rides directly behind Stuart.

Jackson's headquarters' tents can be seen in the right background. The Richard Corbin family, who owned the plantation, has taken advantage of the view from the upper porch to enjoy the exciting event.

To me, this was a memorable moment of pageantry and peace.

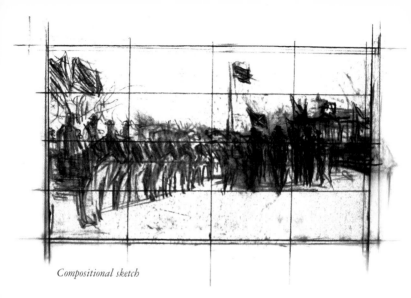

Compositional sketch

Wayside Farewell

MIDDLETOWN, VA.
February 3, 1863

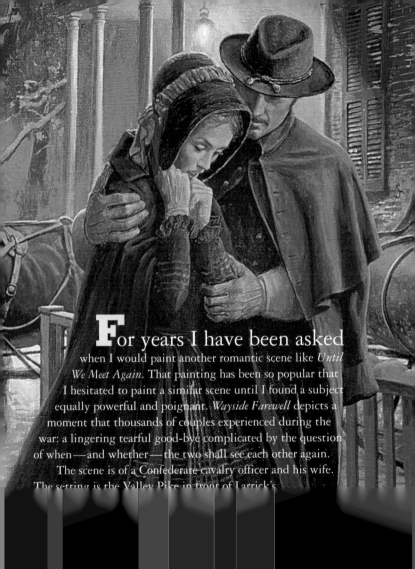

For years I have been asked when I would paint another romantic scene like *Until We Meet Again*. That painting has been so popular that I hesitated to paint a similar scene until I found a subject equally powerful and poignant. *Wayside Farewell* depicts a moment that thousands of couples experienced during the war: a lingering tearful good-bye complicated by the question of when—and whether—the two shall see each other again.

The scene is of a Confederate cavalry officer and his wife. The setting is the Valley Pike in front of Larrick's

Hotel in Middletown, Virginia. The couple were overnight guests at Larrick's—now known as the Wayside Inn—and are saying good-bye in the predawn darkness as the officer's troops wait nearby. An attendant holds a team of horses hitched to a sleigh, which will take the young wife home when her husband and his men depart.

I have enjoyed so many visits to the Shenandoah Valley and the Winchester area that I consider the region to be my "hometown" in the South. Middletown's Wayside Inn is one of my favorite places partly because it is such an interesting-looking structure. I painted the building as I believe it appeared in the 1860s. In the extreme left background are the Sperry house and store, and in the center background is Rickard's Tavern. The sign, lamp post, and gate of the hotel are based on wartime sketches by J. E. Taylor. Professor James I. Robertson Jr. confirmed for me that a four-inch snowfall covered the Middletown region on February 3, 1862, which is the time in which I place the painting.

Countless tender moments like this one occurred throughout the war, and I hope *Wayside Farewell* represents them well.

Figure sketches

Conceptual sketch

Compositional sketch

Wayside Inn as it looks today.

Winter Riders

RALEIGH, N.C.
February 5, 1863

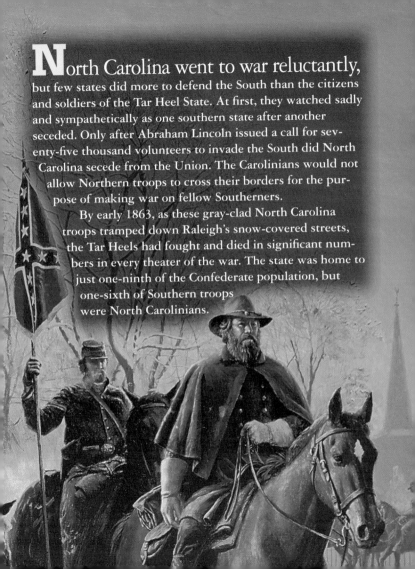

North Carolina went to war reluctantly, but few states did more to defend the South than the citizens and soldiers of the Tar Heel State. At first, they watched sadly and sympathetically as one southern state after another seceded. Only after Abraham Lincoln issued a call for seventy-five thousand volunteers to invade the South did North Carolina secede from the Union. The Carolinians would not allow Northern troops to cross their borders for the purpose of making war on fellow Southerners.

By early 1863, as these gray-clad North Carolina troops tramped down Raleigh's snow-covered streets, the Tar Heels had fought and died in significant numbers in every theater of the war. The state was home to just one-ninth of the Confederate population, but one-sixth of Southern troops were North Carolinians.

This painting originated in 1992 when the North Carolina Museum of History in Raleigh asked to host a one-man exhibition of my Civil War art. After two years and several visits to Raleigh, the concept for *Winter Riders* emerged. Featuring Confederate troops and civilians, it represents the state's major contribution to the war: its people. It also allowed me to focus on a snow scene and an evening theme set near the state capitol—appropriately near the present site of the new museum.

With the help of Raymond Beck, the capitol historian, I learned which shops operated on Fayetteville Street during the war, adding color as well as authenticity to the painting. The owner of the jewelry store, for instance, was John C. Palmer, a Raleigh silversmith, whose handiwork is now part of the museum's collection. The museum's military curator, Tom Belton, provided information on the soldiers' uniforms, equipment, and accouterments.

The capitol and Christ Episcopal Church have changed little in appearance since the war and today look virtually the same as they did in 1863. Even the placement of the street lamps and the lighting in the capitol windows are accurate. In front of the capitol's south façade is sculptor Jean Houdon's statue of George Washington, which still stands in the same spot today. The iron fence, glimpsed just to the left of the horse and wagon, encircled the capitol in the 1860s and today can be seen surrounding Raleigh's city cemetery. The capitol was blanketed with snow on February 5, 1863, so that was the date I chose for this scene.

Flying atop the capitol dome is the Confederacy's first national flag and the North Carolina state flag. The Confederate battle flag was carried by the North Carolina cavalry, thus giving me the opportunity to show all three flags in the same painting.

Compositional sketch

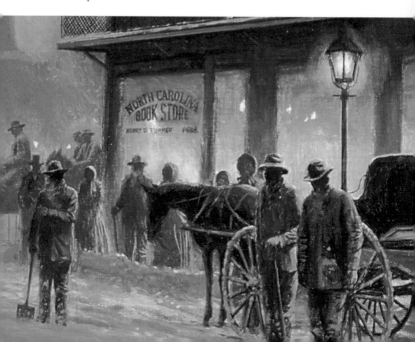

Confederate Sunset

FREDERICKSBURG, VA.

February 1863

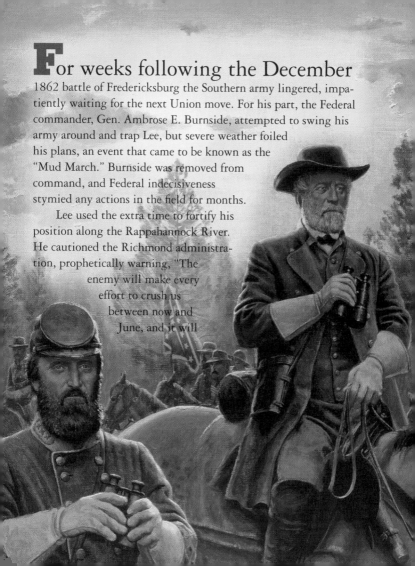

For weeks following the December

1862 battle of Fredericksburg the Southern army lingered, impatiently waiting for the next Union move. For his part, the Federal commander, Gen. Ambrose E. Burnside, attempted to swing his army around and trap Lee, but severe weather foiled his plans, an event that came to be known as the "Mud March." Burnside was removed from command, and Federal indecisiveness stymied any actions in the field for months.

Lee used the extra time to fortify his position along the Rappahannock River. He cautioned the Richmond administration, prophetically warning, "The enemy will make every effort to crush us between now and June, and it will

require all our strength to resist him." The general spent a great deal of time with his lieutenants, bolstering morale, and enjoyed the company of Jeb Stuart, James Longstreet, and Stonewall Jackson at every opportunity.

These early months in 1863 were the last the three commanders spent together. When Federal transports headed down the Potomac, Lee dispatched Longstreet to protect Richmond. Longstreet would rejoin Lee at Gettysburg, but by then the matchless Jackson would be gone.

Lee, Jackson, and Longstreet are the Confederate commanders who fascinate me the most. I decided to paint the three at sunset. I had not done a sunset in any of my Civil War works, so the idea was not only appropriate but very appealing to me. James I. Robertson Jr. affirmed that the three commanders were together several times on staff reconnaissance during early 1863. I chose to place the painting in early February, shortly before Longstreet left for detached duty.

The terrain is typical of the Virginia woodlands near Fredericksburg. The hardwood forest has not yet leafed out and adds a distant, somber tone to the background. Near the Confederate front line, the three commanders observe the distant enemy from a broom-straw clearing amid a sparse stand of Virginia pines.

I thought a golden glow would be appropriate for the scene. While they could not know it at the time, these three exceptional men were in the sunset of their time together. Although Lee's greatest victory still lay ahead, the golden age of Southern glory was beginning to fade.

Mixed media study

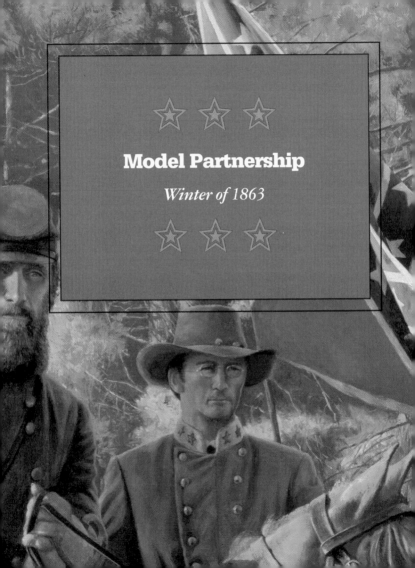

Model Partnership

Winter of 1863

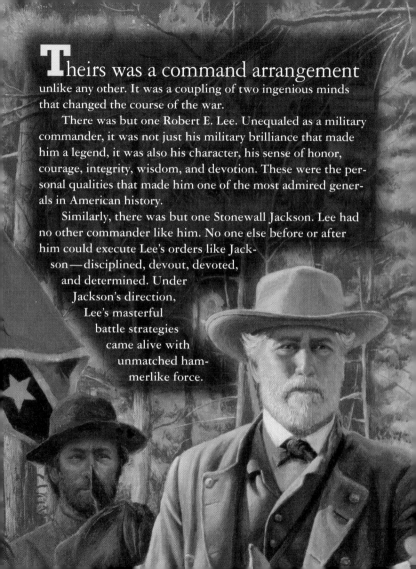

Theirs was a command arrangement unlike any other. It was a coupling of two ingenious minds that changed the course of the war.

There was but one Robert E. Lee. Unequaled as a military commander, it was not just his military brilliance that made him a legend, it was also his character, his sense of honor, courage, integrity, wisdom, and devotion. These were the personal qualities that made him one of the most admired generals in American history.

Similarly, there was but one Stonewall Jackson. Lee had no other commander like him. No one else before or after him could execute Lee's orders like Jackson—disciplined, devout, devoted, and determined. Under Jackson's direction, Lee's masterful battle strategies came alive with unmatched hammerlike force.

During the year in which they worked in tandem, they changed history. They came from different backgrounds, generations, and cultures, but their differences complimented each other, and their similarities bound them in a complex mixture of friendship and respect. Both loved Virginia, graduated from West Point, and fought honorably in the Mexican War. Both were private and humble, but when called upon to defend their homeland they demonstrated unsurpassed skills in the art of war.

Since this was the final painting in the *Legends in Gray* series, I wanted it to be especially memorable. I decided to show Jackson and Lee up close and facing the viewer. The last time I had painted Jackson and Lee in such an intimate setting was years earlier in *The Generals Were Brought to Tears*. In that painting, I featured them in profile. For *Model Partnership*, I chose to show them boldly facing forward, as if confronting an uncertain future with the courage and determination for which they were so well known. I wanted them side by side to emphasize the unique closeness of their working relationship.

Since this scene takes place just months before Jackson's death, I placed them in the late afternoon sun. I wanted them to be lit by the sun's warm glow. I am pleased with the outcome: the sunlight striking Jackson, Lee, and the Confederate battle flag. Staff officers, like supporting characters in a great drama, remain appropriately shadowed. The emphasis in this painting is on the marvelous relationship that made Jackson and Lee a model partnership, that made them *Legends in Gray*.

Mixed media study

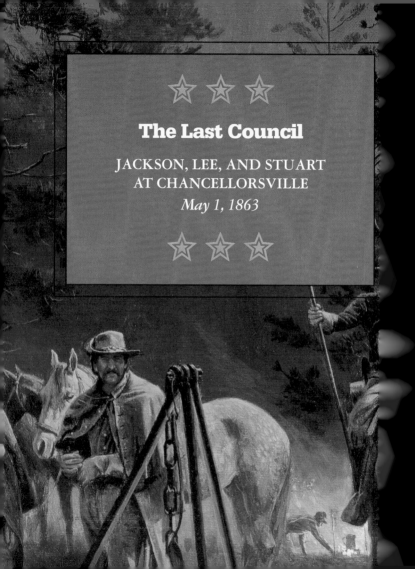

The Last Council

JACKSON, LEE, AND STUART
AT CHANCELLORSVILLE
May 1, 1863

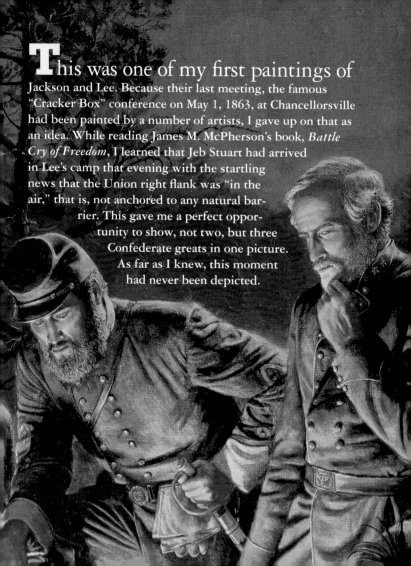

This was one of my first paintings of Jackson and Lee. Because their last meeting, the famous "Cracker Box" conference on May 1, 1863, at Chancellorsville had been painted by a number of artists, I gave up on that as an idea. While reading James M. McPherson's book, *Battle Cry of Freedom*, I learned that Jeb Stuart had arrived in Lee's camp that evening with the startling news that the Union right flank was "in the air," that is, not anchored to any natural barrier. This gave me a perfect opportunity to show, not two, but three Confederate greats in one picture. As far as I knew, this moment had never been depicted.

The lighting proved to be difficult, but the end result was dramatic. The warm firelight contrasted with the chilly moonlight, making the scene perfect for the telling of the story.

The Federals had twice the men and occupied a superior position. Lee and Jackson had been debating their options when Stuart arrived. Because of Jackson's reputation as a strategist, I chose to have him suggesting the planned attack, which would require Lee to divide his force and remain with only fifteen thousand men to confront the main Union force while Jackson marched around the Union flank with more than twenty-eight thousand men. As he contemplates this high-risk strategy, Lee, the great decision maker, is the center of interest. The cavalry in the rear are part of Stuart's entourage who have just ridden in with the news of the Union troop movements.

The gamble paid off, and the battle of Chancellorsville turned out to be Lee's greatest victory. It was also, ironically, his costliest, and the painting's darkness warns of a tragic end.

A few hours after this last council, Jackson was shot accidentally by his own men. He died on May 10, 1863. The battle of Chancellorsville turned out to be Lee's greatest victory as well as his greatest loss.

The Grand Review

BRANDY STATION, VA.
June 5, 1863

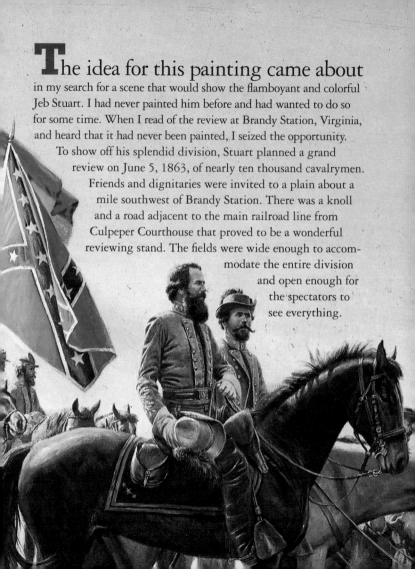

The idea for this painting came about in my search for a scene that would show the flamboyant and colorful Jeb Stuart. I had never painted him before and had wanted to do so for some time. When I read of the review at Brandy Station, Virginia, and heard that it had never been painted, I seized the opportunity.

To show off his splendid division, Stuart planned a grand review on June 5, 1863, of nearly ten thousand cavalrymen. Friends and dignitaries were invited to a plain about a mile southwest of Brandy Station. There was a knoll and a road adjacent to the main railroad line from Culpeper Courthouse that proved to be a wonderful reviewing stand. The fields were wide enough to accommodate the entire division and open enough for the spectators to see everything.

People arrived from Charlottesville and Richmond, and the crowd included most of the town of Culpeper. The train from Richmond that brought Secretary of War George W. Randolph and a large contingent of ladies was parked on the tracks behind the reviewing area.

Based on a trip to the site and maps of the area, I was able to reconstruct the event. The area is now divided by a highway and the knoll is now covered with houses, but the field is virtually unchanged.

For a grand finale the units charged past Stuart and the visitors with a final salute. The troopers went from west to east, with the spectators facing north. The sun in the upper left corner of the painting is coming from out of the west. Stuart is seen on a black charger alongside his aide, Maj. Heros von Borcke, who gave an excellent account of the proceedings that day in his memoirs.

Although Robert E. Lee was not present, his son Rooney was. He can be seen with plumed hat, canteen, and saddlebags directly in back of the unmounted guard. The next mounted officer farther to the right and directly beneath the flying Confederate battle flag is Gen. Fitzhugh Lee, Robert E. Lee's nephew. Next in line is Gen. Wade Hampton, the famed South Carolinian who succeeded Stuart as cavalry corps commander in 1864.

Immediately after the review, the different commands returned to their assigned camps, and Stuart and his aides went back to Culpeper for an evening ball and entertainment. Perhaps the best summation of the review is from von Borcke, who wrote, "One magnificent pageant, inspiring enough to make even an old woman feel fightish!"

Ironically, within forty-eight hours of the grand review, Stuart's cavalry was fighting on this same ground. The battle of Brandy Station was the largest cavalry engagement of the war and marked the beginning of the end of Southern dominance from the saddle.

The Loneliness of Command

GEN. ROBERT E. LEE

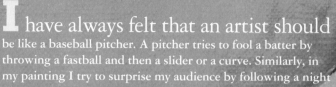

I have always felt that an artist should be like a baseball pitcher. A pitcher tries to fool a batter by throwing a fastball and then a slider or a curve. Similarly, in my painting I try to surprise my audience by following a night scene with a sunlit scene, a complex setting with a simple setting, or an action picture with a still, contemplative one.

After painting *Wayside Farewell*, a very complex scene, I was compelled to think about a more simple composition. I looked at one of the mixed-media paintings I had prepared for my book *Jackson and Lee* and saw that I could develop an oil that would give me the desired effect.

The key to the success of this type of painting is the simplicity of the composition. Without a "great" Lee and a special lighting

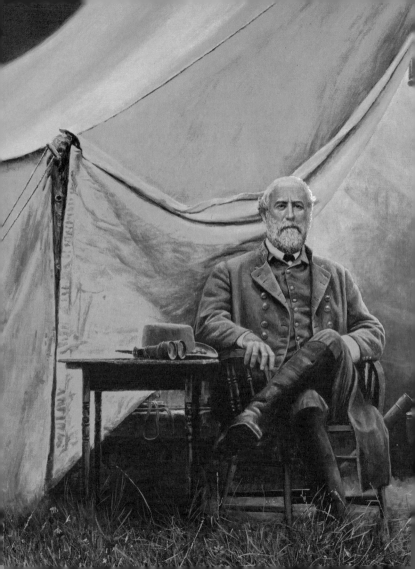

effect, I did not think it would be successful. The composition, lighting, and Lee had worked for me in the "study," so it made the oil that much easier to do.

I have painted Lee many times, but the angle of his head or the lighting is different every time. I solve problems of this type by working with a head sculpture of Lee and lighting it with a flashlight to get the desired lighting effect and angle. Then I do preliminary charcoal sketches. Following these procedures, I ensure that I will paint the best possible Lee I can.

The pose is also important. Here it is designed to capture Lee's dignity as well as the burden of command that the great Confederate general must have felt during virtually every waking moment of the entire war.

Mixed media study

The High Water Mark

GETTYSBURG

July 3, 1863

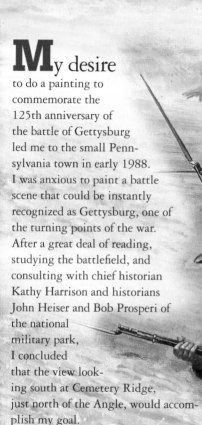

My desire

to do a painting to
commemorate the
125th anniversary of
the battle of Gettysburg
led me to the small Penn-
sylvania town in early 1988.
I was anxious to paint a battle
scene that could be instantly
recognized as Gettysburg, one of
the turning points of the war.
After a great deal of reading,
studying the battlefield, and
consulting with chief historian
Kathy Harrison and historians
John Heiser and Bob Prosperi of
the national
military park,
I concluded
that the view look-
ing south at Cemetery Ridge,
just north of the Angle, would accomplish my goal.

    After two days of fighting, Lee believed
that his assaults on the Union flanks had
weakened the center. Gen. George Pickett's Virginians had just arrived, so on
July 3 Lee directed them toward the

center. After a furious two-hour artillery duel the Union cannon fell silent. Assuming that this meant the Federal artillery was wrecked, Lee gave the order to attack.

Nearly fifteen thousand men in a mile-wide line began marching across a three-quarter mile expanse of open pasture. Entrenched on the opposite ridge behind stone walls, Union soldiers watched as the undaunted Confederates, full of valor, marched forward.

The Union artillery, however, was still intact—Southern aim had been high and wide of the mark. Federal cannon now thundered, deadly accurate at close range. The center held, and the Union flanks folded in to crush the Confederates. Barely half of the fifteen thousand Southerners survived the charge.

In one painting I was able to capture the Union troops firmly entrenched behind the stone wall during Pickett's Charge, the famed Angle, the copse of trees that was the focus of the attack, and the Round Tops in the background. In the right foreground, soldiers of the Twenty-second and Twenty-sixth North Carolina charge headlong into the overwhelming fire of the Fourteenth Connecticut. In the right middle ground, a soldier in a shell jacket and blue pants, with his back toward the viewer, wears an Iron Brigade hat as a trophy taken two days earlier from a fallen Union soldier.

Pennsylvania regiments battle in the Angle in front of the copse of trees with Lewis Armistead's Virginians as the Garibaldi Guard rushes in to reinforce from the left. The cannon from Arnold's battery, firing double canister at close range, take a deadly toll as man after man charges the stone wall. Those who did breach the wall were captured as Union reinforcements arrived. The remaining Confederates withdrew, leaving their fallen comrades to mark the high water mark of the Confederacy.

"It's All My Fault"

GEN. ROBERT E. LEE
AT GETTYSBURG
July 3, 1863

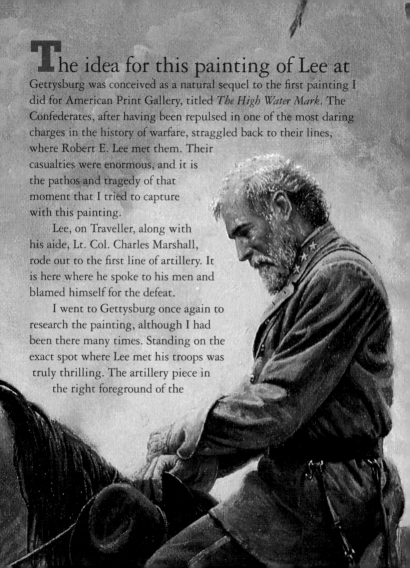

The idea for this painting of Lee at Gettysburg was conceived as a natural sequel to the first painting I did for American Print Gallery, titled *The High Water Mark*. The Confederates, after having been repulsed in one of the most daring charges in the history of warfare, straggled back to their lines, where Robert E. Lee met them. Their casualties were enormous, and it is the pathos and tragedy of that moment that I tried to capture with this painting.

Lee, on Traveller, along with his aide, Lt. Col. Charles Marshall, rode out to the first line of artillery. It is here where he spoke to his men and blamed himself for the defeat.

I went to Gettysburg once again to research the painting, although I had been there many times. Standing on the exact spot where Lee met his troops was truly thrilling. The artillery piece in the right foreground of the

painting is a 10-pound Parrott rifle that still stands at that spot on the battlefield.

I learned that the general did not have his sword but did wear a sword belt. The rest of his uniform and that of Marshall is based on information I found at Gettysburg and in contemporary accounts. Traveller is based on contemporary photographs, as are the likenesses of Lee and Marshall. Marshall's likeness was much more difficult to paint because there are no photographs of him in profile.

To the rear and extreme right of the painting are three artillerymen with the traditional red trim on their uniforms. The private in the foreground holds an artillery guidon. Their expressions reflect the defeat that has become obvious to everyone.

The time is approximately 4:00 P.M. The sun has disappeared because of an incoming storm. With the smoke from the fire of the Spangler barn, which was burning all day, and the dust kicked up by the men and horses, the lighting effect would have been about the way I pictured it here. The wind was from the west, or right of the painting.

I learned about the uniforms and weaponry while painting *The High Water Mark*. The buckle on the butternut soldier helping a wounded, tattered comrade in the left foreground indicates that he is a North Carolinian. Farther back, on the left, are two mounted officers, both wounded. There were only six mounted officers in the original assault, and one of the riderless horses is seen farther to the center in the background. A Virginia regiment's flag is prominent among the few battle flags that were not captured. The rest of the soldiers are struggling and helping each other back to their lines.

I hope this painting brings to life one of the most poignant moments in Confederate history.

Portrait sketch

Confederate Christmas

Each of my paintings seems to come about in a different way. The inspiration for *Confederate Christmas* came from a Civil War etching discovered by Ted Sutphen of American Print Gallery in Gettysburg, my publisher of limited-edition prints.

As I studied the etching, I wondered where the soldiers found the tree. Then I began planning my own painting. Why not show the troops marching through the woods? Why not a snow scene? Why not set the scene at night and add torches

to the march to make the painting more dramatic? In addition to the artillery unit hauling the tree to its camp, why not add some infantry for variety?

The problems and questions an artist encounters and asks himself are endless. Each painting has its own special problems, so the steps from this stage to the finished painting will vary. To do this type of realistic painting requires a great deal of thought and preparation before I even stretch the canvas.

Here, my first step was to prepare some thumbnail sketches—small, crude scribbles—to explore every possibility. I experimented with the soldiers coming toward the viewer, heading away, and in profile. I then developed my thumbnail sketches into the rough compositions on which I based my final painting.

The final scene is full of contrasts: the hint of war conveyed in the soldiers' uniforms and weapons and the white serenity of a snow-covered landscape at Christmastime.

The idea for Confederate Christmas *came from this 1860s etching.*

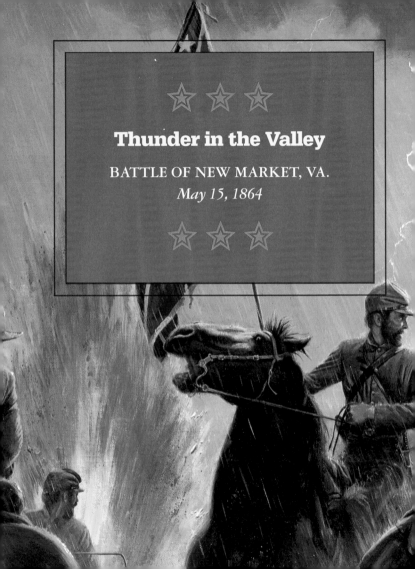

Thunder in the Valley

BATTLE OF NEW MARKET, VA.
May 15, 1864

When I decided to paint the May 15, 1864, battle of New Market, Virginia, I knew I wanted to incorporate three important visual elements. First, the battle occurred during a terrible thunderstorm. Second, more than two hundred cadets from the Virginia Military Institute, almost all of them teenagers, participated valiantly. Third, the Confederate commander, Gen. John C. Breckinridge, was a former vice president of the United States.

I visited the battlefield where park director Ed Merrill and curator Keith Gibson took me step by step through the engagement. I was struck by the charm and beauty of the Bushong house, which still stands at the center of the battlefield.

If I focused on the cadets near the house, they would simply be marching past it in parade-ground fashion, and I knew that image would not make an interesting painting. As I wandered around

the battlefield where Breckinridge had set up his command post, I realized I could show him in conjunction with the VMI cadets and an artillery battery in action near the command position. I could also utilize the lightning as a light source and still feature the Bushong house. I was sure this was the solution to the problem of saying "New Market" in a dramatic and interesting way.

With the battle occurring during a torrential downpour, the main effect I wanted to create was wetness. The rain would have washed the mud off the men and horses as fast as they were being covered with it. I had also never seen a painting of anyone in the rubberized blankets used at the time, so I decided to put one on Breckinridge.

I find the difficulties of fighting a battle under these conditions truly amazing. Imagine trying to keep track of the enemy, keeping your powder dry and your weapon working, and controlling your horse while lightning, thunder, and gunfire filled the air! Even more amazing is that despite these conditions and the fact that the Federals outnumbered them, Breckinridge and his men were victorious.

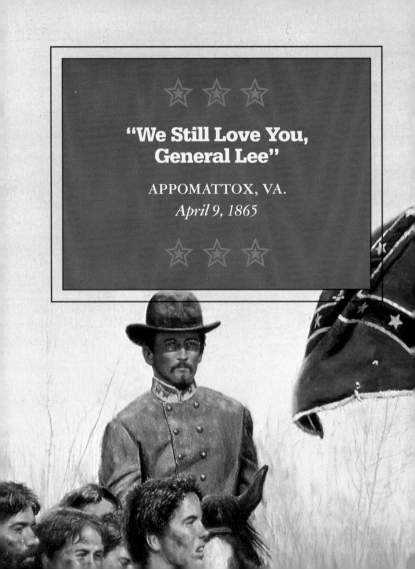

"We Still Love You,
General Lee"

APPOMATTOX, VA.
April 9, 1865

Returning to his camp after meeting with U. S. Grant at Appomattox, Lee rides his beloved Traveller through the Southern lines. He wears a full-dress uniform, sash, and ceremonial sword. He had wanted to look his best for the encounter with Grant, which he had faced with characteristic dignity.

Although defeated, Lee had negotiated generous terms that paroled his men and allowed them to keep their horses. As he rides past them, the soldiers, many with tears in their eyes, cheer and press toward him, touching his leg or even his horse out of affection.

Pausing, Lee told his army, "Men, we have fought the war together, and I have done the best I could for you." He then doffed his hat, uttered a heartfelt good-bye, and returned to his tent. A tattered soldier turned in the ranks and shouted, "We still love you, General Lee!" Even now, more

than a century later, the legacy of the man still evokes strong sentiments from those who study the war.

In 1960, I read Burke Davis's *To Appomattox.* At the time, I was not particularly interested in the Civil War, but I found his descriptions of the surrender and Lee's return to his headquarters very poignant. More than twenty years later I was commissioned to do a painting that would become the logo for the miniseries *The Blue and the Gray.* I became inspired and did a series of paintings on the Civil War that were exhibited at a one-man show at Hammer Galleries in New York City in 1982. One of those paintings was *We Still Love You, General Lee.*

After the show, I moved on to mostly western and Americana themes. Finally, I embarked on a series of epic events in American history, such as the fall of the Alamo, Custer's Last Stand, and the battle of Gettysburg. While I was in Gettysburg, researching the painting that became *The High Water Mark,* I met Ted Sutphen of American Print Gallery. He later began to publish my work as limited-edition prints, including all the paintings in this book.

To make a print of *We Still Love You, General Lee*, I borrowed the original painting from the owner, and I made a number of minor changes to the painting that I felt would improve it. Most artists love to have an opportunity to work on a painting years after they have "finished" it. The print was well received, but I was not satisfied.

I had always wanted to paint a mural. To embark on a very large painting, however, it is necessary to have a finished smaller painting. I chose *We Still Love You, General Lee* for this huge undertaking because I felt it had all the ingredients of composition, color, emotion, and an event of epic proportion. Again I made changes. Thus, I have two finished paintings of Lee at Appomattox. It all goes back to 1960 and *To Appomattox*...and I still have the book!

With special thanks to:

Larry Stone and Ed Curtis of Rutledge Hill Press who originated the idea of twin volumes of my Civil War paintings. Their imagination has brought to fruition *Mort Künstler's Civil War: The South* and its companion book on the North.

Richard Lynch, director of Hammer Galleries in New York City, who gave me my first one-man show in 1977. Nine more shows and a lasting friendship have followed. My appreciation also to Howard Shaw and the rest of the staff at Hammer Galleries.

Ted and Mary Sutphen of American Print Gallery, Gettysburg, Pennsylvania, who published my first Civil War print in 1988. More than sixty-five editions have followed. I treasure their advice and friendship and look forward to our future collaborations.

The myriad of historians, too numerous to mention on this page, who have all been so generous with their time and have enthusiastically shared their expertise and knowledge to ensure the accuracy in my paintings.

Jane Künstler Broffman and Paula McEvoy who continue to run a busy studio with dedication, patience, and understanding. I could not function without them.

And my dear Deborah—wife, partner, consultant, adviser, lover, and best friend, who does everything possible to allow me the most time for my second love, painting.